You're an
Over-the-Hill
Golfer
When...

Other Books by Randy Voorhees

The Little Book of Golf Slang

The Laws of Angling

You Might Be a Golf Nut If . . .

The Laws of Golf

You're an Over-the-Hill Golfer When...

Randy Voorhees

STARK BOOKS

Andrews McMeel Publishing

Kansas City

A MOUNTAIN LION BOOK

ISBN: 0-7407-1524-0

Library of Congress Catalog Card Number: 00-108496

Book composition by Kelly & Company, Lee's Summit, Missouri

For Joan and Charles Voorhees,
my mom and dad.
You've always been the best.

Acknowledgments

I'd like to thank Mark Gola, Joan Mohan, and John Monteleone for contributing to this book. Thanks, too, to Allan Stark for believing in the concept. Lastly, special thanks to my father-in-law, John Hurley, and his pals Nick Cicchino and Amos Hendricks, for serving as inspiration for much of the material herein. See, John, I told you if you kept playing someone would recognize you for your golf.

Introduction

An Over-the-Hill Golfer is one who no longer dreams of great things. He thinks not of conquest, but of survival; not of birdie, but of bogey. He no longer visualizes mighty drives or fist-pumping par saves. He is a gatherer now, where once he was a hunter. He patrols the woods and rough in search of abandoned balls, and plans his round to leave the course in time for the Early Bird Special at the local diner.

At first glance it may not be easy to recognize an Over-the-Hill Golfer, because golf is the one sport where "seasoned citizens," as Harvey Penick referred to them, can compete evenly with comparative youngsters. With precision accuracy off the tee, perfect course management, a rock-solid mental game, and a safecracker's touch around the greens, a senior golfer is a match for any "flatbelly." *Not!* (Any senior who has all those talents will be on your television screen, not at the local muni.) Competitively speaking, an Over-the-Hill Golfer is to the rest of us as the lame wildebeest is to the lion.

Are Over-the-Hill Golfers bad guys? Of course not. We don't yell at them for playing slowly or badly, or for falling asleep over putts. Over-the-Hill Golfers have been to the top of the mount, so they remember. They just don't remember *how*. They deserve our compassion and respect, to be sure. It's just that so much of their behavior is funny. And the clothes they wear! We might as well laugh while we can.

With a little detective work—this book will help—you'll be able to identify those golfers whose shafts aren't as stiff as they once were.

You can use the humor on the following pages to have some fun with Over-the-Hill Golfers you know or to add some spice to a speech you're making at the senior center. Just remember that it's still a helluva lot better to be an Over-the-Hill golfer than a dead one.

You're an Over-the-Hill Golfer When...

Seven A.M. is your idea
of a late tee time.

Your swing isn't strong enough or
long enough to create back pain . . .
but your back hurts anyway.

Whether or not to lay up
is no longer a dilemma.

You can't wait to get
to the 19th hole . . .
to play pinochle.

You don't take dead
aim at the flagstick
because you can't see it.

You won't play with anyone
who doesn't know CPR.

Your spouse doesn't care
how often you play.

Even titanium won't help.

All your bets are settled with dimes.

When you drive,
you're standing a lot closer
to the red tees than the blues.

You enjoy watching the
"young guys" on the senior tour.

Your set contains
all woods.

You've ever fallen asleep
while lining up a putt.

Your best drive produces
responses such as,
"Didn't quite get it all, huh?"

No one asks you for advice
on any part of the game.

You won't play any course that
doesn't offer senior discounts
and a box lunch.

You don't own
two golf balls alike.

You'd rather quit in the
middle of a round than
be late for dinner
(at two-thirty P.M.).

You can no longer
hit the ball far enough
to reach the woods.

After every shot you have to ask,
"Did anybody see it?"

You drive the cart with both hands on the wheel and your foot on the brake.

You wear a helmet because you couldn't
hear someone yelling "Fore!" if
they were sharing your pants.

The thought of shooting
your age isn't so ridiculous.

You attend reunions of Arnie's Army.

You realize you're never going to break 80.

The beer cart doesn't even slow down for you.

You're no longer embarrassed to play with your wife. In fact, you must play with her because she knows all the dosages.

You get into a heated debate over who drank the last V8.

You can't position the ball off your left foot because you can't *see* your left foot.

Flatbelly becomes your favorite term of derision.

Your rounds begin and end with Ben Gay.

Carrying your bag is not an option.

You use your putter to get
the ball *out* of the hole.

No shot is too short for a fairway wood.

You play more than ever,
but never on weekends.

You can remember when
woods were made of wood.

You play golf in Florida—
in the summer—
and you're still cold.

You remember Jack Nicklaus
as a fat guy with a crewcut.

You own spikes older
than Tiger Woods.

The drive to the course is more nerve-wracking than the drive from the first tee.

You refer to your age as being "somewhere along the back nine."

You own your own golf cart
and you and your spouse's
names are painted on the side.

Your putter is longer
than your driver.

Your wife took your ball retriever
because she doesn't want you
to go near the water.

You can remember when the
40-foot oak guarding the
12th green was just a seedling.

You require assistance to put your tee in the ground.

You always leave the course
in time to get home before dark.

Younger golfers fight not to
be in the group behind you.

Walking to and from your cart
is the most exercise you get all day.

You only meet new golfers
when a member of your group dies.

Your claim to fame is being
the best *living* golfer from your
high school graduating class.

You often lay up . . .
on par 3s.

You wouldn't dream of playing
more than eighteen holes in a day.

You no longer play golf with Democrats.

You never drive off the cart path.

You know you once made a
hole in one but you can't
remember the details.

You report gambling winnings
on your tax return because
you're afraid not to.

You forget your score before you get home.

You bring your driver to
the pitch-and-putt course.

You call the ranger "sonny."

You're always picking up discarded tees and balls. (You're now a gatherer, not a hunter.)

The starter trusts you enough
to allow you to play before paying.

No one threatens to beat you up
for playing slow or cutting in.

You often tell the maintenance
men that they've done a
"fine job of mowing."

You look forward to playing
temporary tees and greens.

You can't remember the
last time someone told you
to slow down your swing.

You have problems
keeping your head *up*.

You'd rather have a
new garbage disposal
than a new driver.

You think the club pro is
too young to know anything.

You actually use the blue gel in the locker room.

You can't pass by a bunker
without doing a little "gardening."

A case of the yips would improve your putting.

You put your glasses on to read a putt.

You work part time as a ranger . . .
and you take the job seriously.

You consider a husband-wife
tournament a "night out."

You own a motorized pull cart.

You'd rather sweep the walkway
than watch the Masters tournament.

You recognize the starter as your old paperboy.

You own a bumper sticker that says
I'D RATHER BE IN MYRTLE BEACH.

You send postcards from
your golf destinations.

Between nines, you go for the
vegetable sandwich instead of a hot dog.

Your golf sweaters all have buttons
because you can't get those
vests over your head.

Your clubs don't fit
because you've shrunk.

You fire your caddie
because he refuses to
change your diaper.

You yell at another golfer
for driving his cart too fast.

Your fantasy includes reaching
a par 5 without hitting your
three-wood more than five times.

Bob Hope is among the
golfers you admire most.

You're most famous for
being the man who stalked
Babe Didrikson Zaharias.

You once spray-painted Harry Vardon's
name on a highway overpass.

You knew Old Tom Morris
before Young Tom Morris was born.

You wear an ID bracelet
instead of a copper bracelet.

You've ever had to pop a
nitroglycerin pill after sinking
a particularly important putt.

You've ever passed a
kidney stone in a bunker.

You need help
climbing out of bunkers.

You're the only one at
the nude beach with a
sand wedge in his hand.

You loan clubs,
then can't remember
who you gave them to.

You were there when Byron Nelson
won the first of his record-setting
eleven consecutive victories.

You think the movie
Caddyshack is stupid.

You worry more about the
yips than erectile dysfunction.

All your playing partners
address you as "Mister."

Your second honeymoon was all about "resort golf" instead of sex.

You often comment about "how good Arnold Palmer looks."

Your previous set of clubs
included a brassie, a niblick,
and a mashie.

Your home course is ensconced
in a gated community.

You own yellow golf pants and
aren't afraid to wear them.

You duck behind the trees
to "find relief" a lot
more often than before.

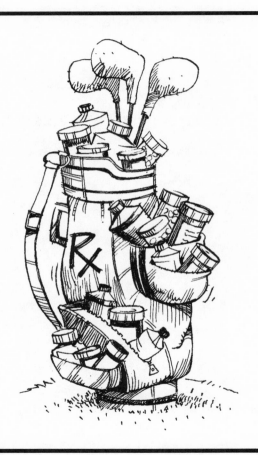

Your golf bag doubles as a medicine cabinet.

You need a running start to reach
the surface of an elevated green.

You start wearing dark socks
with your golf sandals.

You frequently forget where you placed your ball marker.

Antique dealers inquire about the availability of your clubs.

Your car is large enough
to accommodate *two*
foursomes and their clubs.

It's hard to tell where the
leather grip stops and
your hands begin.

The club installs a compass on your golf cart.

Tennis is (physically) out of the question.

You've had every lie and every putt
on the course at least five times.

At the driving range,
a large bucket of balls
is out of the question.

The police often help you
find your car after the round.

The bartender at the 19th hole
checks your blood pressure
instead of your ID.

You're the oldest person on the golf course . . .
on a weekday morning.

You receive a gift subscription to
Senior Golfer magazine . . . from
your granddaughter . . . who paid
for it with her own money.

You can remember when golf tournaments
and *Shell's Wonderful World of Golf*
were broadcast in black and white.

You bring your trophy wife to the club
for the other members to admire.

You're constantly talking about
how long you used to be.

You're no longer afraid of lightning,
because you "could use a good jolt."

You can remember when
nearly every course had caddies—
and they were affordable.

Someone plays the exploding ball trick
on you and the ball doesn't even break.

You couldn't care less about how much time
your wife is spending with the club pro.

You can afford every new club on the market,
but you've finally figured out that
the clubs don't make the man.

No one questions you
for improving your lie.

You can afford to play Pebble Beach
but would rather go to
Branson (Missouri).

Your scores are rising almost
as fast as your cholesterol level.

You're suddenly afraid to make
sacrilegious remarks after
hitting a bad shot.

Your belt and golf shoes
are both white.

You use the Lawrence Welk
headcover for your driver.

You're referred to as a
"pretty good putter for your age."

Everyone in your regular
foursome wears a nametag.

All the entries on your list of
"100 courses to play before
I die" are crossed out.

You can't remember
how to get from the first
green to the second tee.

You treat each round as though
it might be your last.

Your playing partners
complain about how
slow you drive the cart.

Your hearing aid frequently
falls out as you bend over
to tee up your ball.

You can remember when the
book *The Official Rules of Golf*
was just a short story.

Famed golf course architect
Pete Dye is working on
a design for your gravesite.

Directions to your home include
"a driver and wedge from
the shuffleboard court."

You would drive more than
fifty miles to get a good deal
on secondhand golf balls.

You've ever purchased clothes
because they looked good
on Sam Snead.

You've switched to balata balls because you can't hit a ball hard enough to cut the cover.

You hit yard sales for all your "new" equipment.

You scan bunkers with your metal detector.

You're not embarrassed to
use striped range balls
on the golf course.

You stuck a tee behind
your ear and short-
circuited your hearing aid.

You save your oldest, grungiest balls for water holes.

You always forget where you parked the cart.

Your teeth are cut from the
same wood as your tees.

They no longer check your ID
when you ask for the senior rate.

You're amused rather than outraged
when someone cheats you.

You no longer vacation in
Myrtle Beach because it's
"culturally deprived."

You walk so slow that you can
actually make time stand still.

You seriously contemplate on
which hole you wish to die.

Wearing a visor means risking
a serious sunburn on your head.

You're always decrying the
poor manners of younger golfers.

Other golfers often say to you, "At least it was straight."

Scores become less important than survival.

You can't put on or take off
your spikes without sitting down.

Your back goes out replacing a divot.

You store tees and ball markers
in your face wrinkles.

You have to tell your children when
and where you'll be golfing and
what time you expect to be home.

You choose which courses to play
based on how short and flat they are.

You have to soak your feet between nines.

A cat tries to bury you in a bunker.

All of your doctor's emergency
numbers are on file in the pro shop.

Your clubhouse conversations are
more about being "up to par"
rather than making par.

Your wife routinely outdrives you . . .
from the same tee.

You can throw the ball farther than you can hit it.

You don't have enough energy to take mulligans.

You have to stop more than once
to catch your breath between putts.

You refer to Bill Murray as a "smart aleck."

You buy your golf clothes at Sears.

You appreciate slow play as an opportunity for napping.

Before every shot you ask yourself,
"What would President Ford do here?"

You play at the same time, on the same course,
with the same people every day.

You hit all your clubs the same distance.

You can measure your club-head
speed with an hourglass.

You complain about the price of tees.

You couldn't care less about a golf course's impact on the environment.

You can't remember the last time you were invited to play through.

You use an umbrella
rain or shine.

At the 19th hole, you volunteer
to be the designated driver.

You get chastised for snoring during another player's backswing.

You can't remember the last time you
played with someone who still has a job.

You no longer care what
your swing looks like.

You clean your clubs and change your grips even when they don't need it.

You would rather play bingo.

You need reading glasses to fill out your scorecard.

You *really haven't* ever played this bad before.

You warn your caddie about the evils of smoking.

Your backswing doesn't reach
perpendicular, let alone parallel.

You played golf in Hawaii
before it was a state.

You're always tidying up
the ground under repair.